Ships That Go Nowhere

A POETRY COLLECTION

Evelyn Avila

Published by Evelyn Avila
First Edition: May 2024

eeviepoetry.com

ISBN: 979-8-9905649-0-9

Dedicated to Rosa.
She kept her home,
upkept her home.
Until the end.

CONTENTS

THE ONES THAT ARE WRECKED

THE ONES MADE OF PAPER

THE ONES AT WAR

THE ONES THAT NEVER LEAVE THE HARBOR

THE ONES THAT ALMOST MAKE IT

THE ONES SAILING IN THE DARK

THE ONES IN STILL WATERS

THE ONES THAT ARE WRECKED

sink the quickest

california dreams

You saw her walk by us on the way to dinner
Saw her again as we headed home
Guess you couldn't help yourself,
Said I should make a friend
Made me ask for her number
So you could see her again

I liked her a lot, first friend in the new city
Drinks at brunch
Her voice
Her laugh
All pretty
She was sunshine and she told me about
Her mother
Her father
Her brother
She never asked about me
I came from the wrong coast
All rain and drab, the wrong sea
I didn't mind, I had company

But you and her
Giggling to yourselves
Inside jokes
Setting up my bookshelf
She would ask me about you
What you would like to do

In and out of the bedroom
I thought it was girl talk
I never had girl talk
And I would talk
About you
How you found me, how you loved me
The pain you went through to take care of me
How I gave you what you wanted most
To pack up and leave the wrong coast

It was the easiest decision I ever made

But you and her
Cat and mouse for three whole months
Innocently flirting, innocent hand brush
I'd watch from the patio how she'd run her
fingers through your hair
It was too long for her taste
So you had it trimmed
Despite my preference
You claimed it got in the way
So I had nothing to say
I couldn't accuse you
You wanted me to have a friend,
A friend who was always with us
At our dinners, dates, and lunches
You just couldn't escape her as a topic of

conversation
But I had to believe
You wouldn't rip up our california dreams
Watching sunsets, picnics at the beach
With a glass of wine, cheese, and me
Because I'm not that bad
I make you laugh
And you once told me
Your love for me was enough
To ease the pain of your past
Plain Jane with an honest heart
No objections, I'll play any part

With love and patience
We made it through so many things

nowadays
I try not to think about
the words in your best man's speech
about how you two met, fell in love
sharing sunsets at the beach
nowadays
I try not to think about
her hands in your hair, your mouth on hers
an image ingrained deep in my soul
you had just broken up with me,
not even a week
and she was my friend first,
wasn't she?

and foolish me running to her thinking,
wishing, desperately hoping that maybe she
could change your mind, that this thought of a
life without you could be left behind
so I ran
ran up her apartment stairs
couldn't wait for the elevator
couldn't wait a second later
and there you were
and there she was
keys on the floor
hands never made it to the door
entangled
arms around one another
no more hiding
no need for cover
and the next day she would swear to me it was
the first time
and the next day she would ask me to forgive
her
and the next day she would block my number
leave my messages undelivered
and twelve months later
the years we spent together
erased from a drunk man's story
about the purest love he's ever known
who I was and what I meant to you
didn't make the cut
in the story of your california dream

gossip on mango street

little tuft of white hair pokes out from a brand
new pickup truck
whole family had our noses to the window
we eye him up and down, the new gringo
mom says

seems neighbor's got a new roommate

I say

he's my dad's age

mom says

that could've been your dad
when she was slinking around here
asking for favors,
cause her husband's long gone
and she needs a new man with papers
to take care of her and her three little kids,
the bills and the pickle jar lids

I tell mom she's exaggerating
my old man is a faithful man
would never think to leave us
for a tighter fit and a bigger bust
but mom says you can never be too sure

for a faithful man there's always a cure

I roll my eyes, but feel a little tug inside
then shrug it off
just another unsettling feeling to hide

blank 3

how do you know she is enough
to ensure it is like I never happened?
and what's the name of that pill you took?
so I can take it too and never feel your absence
do I get to mourn the person that you were?
or is this who you've always been?
asleep next to me and yet so distant
manifesting this woman into existence
is she really the love of your life
or just another interim?
do you blame me for letting it happen?
is there a part of you that wished I had stopped it?
the last time you said you loved me
did you mean it or did you say it out of habit?
do you have love for me still
but just love her more?
do you know I spend my nights alone
on our bathroom floor?

is this how it's always going to be?
I have questions for you
and you have none for me

ship and sea

she took it all
not just my lover but also my dreams
I'm no longer the main character in my own memories

it's her scent that lingers
in every scene with you
so subtle I never noticed before
and if I think back hard enough
I see it was never me
she stands in my place
whereas I am just a bystander

with her
your demeanor is different
you beam
you are a ship and she is the sea

and your eyes
that so constantly failed to meet mine
naturally lock onto hers

she's your whole world

if

if I were the leaves beneath your feet
instead of the girl on her knees
you might have stepped over me more
carefully

if I were the gum on your shoe
instead of the girl who loved you
you might have given it more thought

if I were the maggots that feast
on your discarded breadcrumbs
or the aphids on the cherry plum
the green of the pond scum
dust beneath the drum
or just anyone

else

you might have let me live in peace

karma

Sometimes karma doesn't get the ones that've done you wrong
You'll sit in a coffee shop, take a bite out of a croissant and give it another go, beg silently to the universe to throw you a bone
Wednesday's been a little rough but you've still picked yourself up

Haven't you done enough?

But you get no reply, you get no sign
Instead you pick up your phone
And scroll and scroll
And it's all good news
For someone else
And you stumble into their picture perfect life
The one they cut you out of with precision
With scissors and blood and fucked up decisions
And you see they're doing better than they've ever done before,
Seems they did you wrong
Then claimed some reward
You try to put in a complaint with the universe's karma department cause everyone knows it shouldn't work this way
But they don't really have a system in place
Just a busy ringtone, a "rate your experience" survey, and a billion people on hold

the you I knew

the you I knew would never hurt me
you were someone I felt lucky to know
always friend first, lover second

and yet it was you who gave me this wound
no amount of tears could seal
big gash in my little soul
I patch it up with minuscule promises
and take it a day at a time
hoping one day I reach my goal

I don't know how you are
just assume you're at the end of a champagne bottle
just assume your life after me is one big adventure

and I wish I could wish bad things for you
I wish I could feel the rage and lash out
pile it on to you
crush you with the feelings that crush me
but I know they won't carry the same weight on you
my efforts would remain fruitless
because I can't hurt you
I can't reach you

aphrodite

my aphrodite loves me
but she does not trust me to stay, says she has
booked the first ticket on the morning train
says she will pine for me, long for me
whisper my name to the wind
knowing I will do the same

I beg her not to leave us to this fate
she says she's not leaving it to fate at all
it is better this way
to forever encapsulate this feeling
means every memory remains unspoiled
and us self-sabotaging cynics can do nothing
to destroy it

I rip her ticket in two
Don't you know I'll change my nature for you?
Aphrodite I love you. You are the most beautiful–
but she only twists her face in anger and
before I can finish exclaims,
Most beautiful? Most beautiful?
What good does that do?
Why have I always been second in my father's eyes
Beauty has not bought me a place in his new life
He would die for his youngest, pull down the moon
and stars for his new wife

And I?
I am but an afterthought
Most Beautiful? Most Beautiful?
I am most beautiful until your eyes drift towards
something new
Most beautiful until my temper catches you
off guard
Most beautiful until you are shit-faced at the bar
Whispering most beautiful, most beautiful to the
next thing you catch between your paws

I am defeated
her eyes signal this decision is set in stone
still I try, I whisper gently

Aphrodite please. That is not me.

but she does not believe me
she throws at me charts, statistics, anecdotes
piles of research and notes
my last plea:

Aphrodite won't you take a chance on me?

but it is futile
and so all of the cheaters and all of the liars
have taken my Aphrodite from me,
filled the world with their dawdling
uncertainty and left me with nothing

who were you

Who were you?
Shuffling at my doorstep, holding my secrets
in the crook of your neck
Dazzling smile, winter boots, I'd wait for you
Who were you?
Pushed to the edge of my memory in self
defense, now I can't place you anymore
Just see pieces of myself crestfallen
on the bedroom floor
Who were you?
Feels like I knew you for more than a lifetime,
knew the path of your life more than mine
I remained lost in the strands of your hair,
your smell, as I followed you until the end,
a destination called nowhere
Who were you?
That you found it so easy to love me then leave
me, to both hold and deceive me, to kiss away
the bad dreams, give me peace and sanity
then make my nightmares a reality
Who were you?
That you epitomized the word romance for me
Showed me butterflies were a real thing
Showed me love could be a real thing
Who were you?
Just a story I tell
One I no longer remember well

nothing

You were nothing when you met me
And to nothing you will return
When you leave me stranded on our front porch

Divorce papers amidst fiery affairs
You must think you're on top of the world
Setting ablaze a home that was never good
enough for you, barricading the doors and
windows to keep me inside
You'll cash out the insurance payment to pay
for your new life
Pitying looks from the neighbors
You'll say you found strength in your new wife
And together you'll buy a house in the
neighborhood with the good schools, never
missing the fixer upper without the rules
But someday it'll click
When your smile falters as you pass the salad
and the breadsticks
How you got everything you ever wanted
And it still feels small and squalid
Because you may never miss me
But you'll miss the way I made you feel
You'd close your eyes and I'd hold you tight
And that's when you knew you could be
anything

alone in the garden

alone in the garden, I sit by the frog pond
my brother and his new wife's guests are all
inside the venue, avoiding the thick blanket of
humidity, avoiding misery and her company

sitting still for an eternity,
a frog finally comes and joins me
I say a meek hello
it does not say hello back, doesn't respond with
a joke and a laugh or put me on true love's path
a frog is a frog
can a frog be a friend?
I look around, and seeing no one, I pretend
start telling the frog about how my plus one
didn't show

He's out there planning a wedding of his own. I'm not sure I believe in weddings, never seen one with a happy ending. Doubt it would've made a difference, doubt it would've made him stay. Even if it was the end of the world and I was the last girl on Earth, he'd have found a way to absolutely crush my soul, break my heart, leave me with only mind and bones

the frog only blinks at me
I let out a sigh
then take a moment to be honest

I think more terrifying than the end of the world is this notion I've had since childhood about two lovers never being able to make it work. Years of building a life together, gone in an instant cause your lover bumped into a new commitment. Years of promising to love each other unconditionally, disintegrating slowly cause you woke up one morning in your heart knowing you've been lying for months. It's not unconditional love. What if I find the one? What if they love me every day of their life and it's not enough. Because it's only a matter of time, right? Love will always change into something different, become small, become insignificant. Because time takes it all, not just the heartbreak and the hurt, but the love and the memory of the one pivotal moment in life when these two lovers were sure that all they'd ever want in the world would be each other.

broken-hearted in the garden,
I seem to have been forgotten
so I wait for the little frog to leave, like they all
do, to resume my melancholic pursuits
and for a second the little thing seems to
contemplate it,
but it decides to stay and sit with me
and now I'm not alone in the garden

some broken stairs

I fell down again
It was those damn stairs again
My ex-husband was supposed to fix them
He got paid to fix things for other people
I didn't have money of my own
Cause there's no paycheck for raising kids and
making sure his shirt buttons are properly
sewn
Or for keeping the floors fabuloso clean
And changing up the recipes
So he didn't eat just rice and beans
Had to wash his sheets
And dirty underwear
Never asked for love
Just fix the damn stairs!

But that made me a nagging woman
The ol' ball and chain
Too wrinkly and plump
For his new pay grade
I didn't mind the affair,
The late night work hours
Meant I could take the hour shower
Without him reprimanding me
About how the water bill is so high
While she orders new outfits
On what's supposed to be our dime

But I took the little wins
And just pulled out the oxiclean to rub on the lipstick between his shirt seams
And turned up the volume on the TV
And when I was done with the day's work
I'd sit and relax
Cause there was no need to use my hands late at night
To make him tea and massage his thighs

He's twice as old as her
Didn't surprise me he wanted the divorce
Tried to put her in my house
And extract me, the little old louse
Said I was a gold digger
Rallied up his friends
Tried to throw mud my way
Saying I never worked a day
But I didn't give a shit
Cause those were my hands on the sparkling windows
My hands on the spotless fan
My hands on the dirty diapers
I disposed of in the trash can
Menial tasks
Day after day
Someone had to do it

Someone had to stay
Not everyone can go
Make it out in the world
Find a husband
That knows your worth

So he got his divorce
And I kept my home,
Upkept my home
For when the grandkids come
They come and see me here
And when death comes
It comes and greets me here
And compliments my choice of linen
Says it's one of the nicer homes it's been in

THE ONES MADE OF PAPER

sink on their own

the girl with the rabbit tattoo

I danced with you when no one else would
Secrets and theories,
Don't fall for the girl with the rabbit tattoo

You burned the tip of my tongue,
Taught me to play a game meant for no one
Somehow you reveled in the misery
Brought upon both you and me

In time I started to feel it too
Your toxic bloom, my greatest muse
I couldn't wash away the feeling you soaked
me in
Heads turned at every corner
I wore my new color with pleasure

I lie awake sometimes
Knowing where it all went wrong
In my head I play your somber song
To reminisce short lived bliss
And ease a lifelong sadness

In my version of events you open the door
Don't leave me rain-soaked
Cackle at my stupidity
Of course you haven't forgotten me
I'm all you ever think about

You take me in your arms
And it is like it always was
Lips on skin
Hands where hands belong

plume blue

I asked for an explanation,
you only gave an excuse
I wrote you thousands of letters,
a fruitless pursuit
And if I could escape you I would
But I see myself reflected in every word you
choose
You've made me your fool

blank 13

I was young, I was in love
The wind told me to be cautious
But it did not tell me what to be cautious of

twin flame

Hey twin flame
I thought you and I were the same
So why did you try to consume me
Act like you never knew me
And then stabbed me in the back
Right where your lips once met me

I closed my eyes
and ran my hands through your hair
I closed my eyes
and you were no longer there

You took the crown I kept on my bedside table
And didn't have the courtesy to leave a note
You probably tell yourself I should have known

Did it anger you?
That all you schemed for
To me was a paperweight at best
Something that if you had only asked
I would have taken the poison from your lips
And laid at your feet to rest
Cause there's a thousand and one ways to be
king

You didn't have to marry him

how to fold a paper ship

Step 1. Give your heart to someone.
Step 2. Have them break it.
Step 3. Repeat.

I know it doesn't make sense
But we're still repeating it
aren't we?

starstruck

you used my words to tell the world how
much she means to you
and spun a record of half-loves and half-truths
you smile coyly as they ask for the name of
your muse
but you've made it all up
don't they know?
you're the girl that doesn't know how to love

I like to think I see right through you
but the truth is even I never knew you
I think of this as I lay awake late at night
to see your name in flashing lights
and listen between the lines, the extent of my
insignificance to you

I wrote you a letter

I wrote you a letter
that I folded into a paper ship shape
the day you crossed the line
and we were never the same again

I let it set sail
one rainy afternoon
after our time together had long passed
and willed it to get to you

A simple phone call could have sufficed
but the words I wished to say to you
were unable to take form on my lips
so they floated down
down into the sewer instead

she writes it all down

she writes it all down
from the color of your eyes
to the details on your gown
makes love stories out of your misery
knows what she did wrong and how to fix it
but lets it all burn
because if it doesn't hurt, it doesn't sell
and if it's not authentic, it's not done well

she's written the end before you ever even met
and she plays her part perfectly
to evoke sympathy for the loss of the truest
love she's ever known
make them all believe another set of star-
crossed lovers fell victim to their destiny
but truthfully,
you were just kindling for her poetry

penelope

penelope's got a gun in her four thousand dollar leather baby blue prada bag she got from her mom

penelope thinks it's fun when she kisses me at the bus stop before she gets picked up by her porsche driving hunk

he's a little dumb, put the ring at the bottom of a bottle of rum she'll never finish
cause she's drunk on me and the minute I'm all dried up she's got another lined up

penelope's the cynical little firecracker you can't let go of
cause she burns but that's just the thing you want more of

penelope knows I'm in love, she tugs and tugs, bites her tongue, until all my secrets are spilled
and I'm nothing but guts on the bathroom floor
and there isn't anything she wants to take anymore

telenovelas

secret lover meet me at five
behind the old hickory barn

secret lover meet me at nine
at the festival of lights

secret lover meet me at midnight
at the lake underneath the full moon's light

Little notes scatter at my feet
Covered in my scent, my chicken scratch writing
I see his eyes burning red, angry
It's fiction I tell him
All fiction
Part of an idea
Something I once thought I wrote

Why can't you see
It's nothing but fantasy
Nothing in real life is that romantic
It's summer
Can't visit the lake so late
Mosquitoes will have my flesh before any
secret lover takes the bait

I crack a smile
He doesn't like my joke

Well what was I to know
You'd betray everything for a few lumps of
gold
You carved your space in me
Then hid behind right and wrong
Ensuring only I burned at the stake
Blamed the stableboy like a coward
Said you found us sneaking around
Now the stableboy is graveyard bound
And my fate is sealed
So goodbye to picking dandelions in the spring
field
And making love underneath the harvest
moon

Do these affairs always end so soon?

Oddly enough,
You seem to have forgotten
How you left your morals at the door of
another man's bedroom
Burned your book of codes on the fire between
my legs
Reckless,
You sold your heart to me
You didn't think it was worth anything
Only good for cashing in on easy starving
women

Foolish enough to think you'd take them away
From the loveless land they once thought they could endure
It's okay, take up a glass, cheer to our corn maze days
Celebrate now before these memories come back to haunt you
My death will be swift, I'll make sure of it
As I try climbing down this ivory tower myself
Becoming another story on his bookshelf
You'll bring flowers to my gravestone
Laugh at me, say I should have known
But in time you too will succumb to the wound
Brought forth by this self-inflicted solitude
You will lament the way you caused our paths to part
The day you realize no one will ever love a man without a heart

dream crushers

the cruelty of my dreams
had me nipping at my tongue
all night long
and I felt the pain
but I couldn't wake
my mind, addicted to endless screenings of
you, walking away, always walking away, a
never-changing ending permanently ingrained
oh my mind's stuck in a loop
directs the whole show
but can't manifest peace in a nicely packaged
wish fulfilled lifetime-esque dream

it's always just us sitting on a cliff's edge
two parked cars at the end of a winding road
and I know the speech by heart
but what always hurts the most
is the lack of remorse
I look into your eyes
hoping to find something different every time
a smidgen of doubt, an ounce of regret, a
wavering in your gaze I can misinterpret

but nothing is ever there

your side of the story

I don't know what tomorrow brings
This is the only real moment for me
Because you can say this won't work out long
term
Pull out the charts, compare our life goals
And sure you're a numbers girl
You like accounting
Taking accountability
But just look at me for a second
Look at me and breathe
Look and see my future
Look and see how I'll always love you
Unconditionally
And you say I want more
Always more
But I can never get enough of you
And you say you can't break yourself in two
Can't be the woman you want to be
And the woman who spends all her time with
me
But I'm not trying to sink your ship
So stop painting me as the villain
Cause I want you to achieve your dreams
Even at the expense of me

So do it, walk all over me
As long as you know
When you wear the glitter and the gold
When you are where you want to be
That thousands of miles away there's this house
Where your laugh rang through these halls
And your fingertips traced these walls
And every moment you told the world you wanted to be alone
You ran here, you ran home
So you can shout it out
Shout it to anyone who'll listen
That our stars were misaligned
Go on confuse what is and what isn't
Because I didn't have to read the stars
To know how I wanted to write my destiny
To know I always wanted you close to me
So take pen to paper
Write your narrative
Write, write, re-write, and overwrite
Put new blank pages over you
Truth's ink always bleeds through

summer days

I remember the day I left my sister's wedding
to go sit in the sun with you
your head was in my lap as your fingers
fiddled with the fringe of my lilac dress
you asked me what I was thinking,
wasn't it kind of an important day
I said I had enough of feeling invisible
and I didn't believe in that stuff anyway
there's like five different ways I see it ending
or maybe they'll get their forever and end up
like my parents
who only last because they've never had a real
conversation
no really,
my mom told me that's the secret
you laughed then cut right through me,
cut right through me when you asked
if I would ever consider marrying you
my heart stopped,
the half a second I allowed it to want
I shook my head,
refused to answer, mumbled something about
how that's not funny
But you always knew
I would do anything for you

You took so much from me
and sometimes I'm bitter about it, sure
But truthfully, I just wish you had taken me
whole
No need for promises, no need for jewels
Just the knowledge that I was yours

graceful, patient, and effortless

I want to be as graceful
As her fingers on this page
Leaving a trail of touch
On these words
I refuse to let go

I want to be as patient
As the rain the day I met her
Soaked my socks, my heart
Thoroughly
The moment she crossed my path
No ray of light in sight
From the beginning,
I stood no chance

I want to be as effortless
As her body
Turning away from me
Over and over again
As if I were nothing

THE ONES AT WAR

succumb to their wounds

better man

she's waited centuries for you to become a
better man
you got the wheel down then made fire rain
from the sky
you tinker with the world, shape it in your
image
robust and indifferent

she's draped over the chaise lounge so
meticulously
you pause for half a second, thinking you'll get
to her needs eventually
sometime hopefully, before she stumbles into
someone else's generosity
and gets it in her head that leaving you was
always an option
she just wants to talk with you
you get her the wrong four-legged pet instead

she's in the ivory tower you built for her
practicing poetry, weaving stories
she closes her eyes and for a second she's in a
smaller place
where cold stone does not brush her face and
warm ash stains her fingertips
there are no luxuries in this home
but the fire lives

blank 24

little angry eyes
peer at me from afar
he has taken my spirit
and put me in a jar

iterations

you're just another iteration
of the same type of storm
I refuse to shelter from
chaotically golden

so when you pull out a diamond ring
as your emotional affair turns one year old
and you don't understand why that's not
romantic
why do I contemplate saying yes anyway
just so I never have to worry about it again?

your words are lovely enough, little band-aids
to insecurities we don't talk about much
and I think it's charming how you cover up
your trail of lies with speeches of love and
trust
yes I do, I do think I can live passive
aggressively beside you forever

because you love me so tepidly
I'll never get burned
and your eyes never linger on me
so what's there to hide from
and if it's you holding me back
I never build something of my own
to keep me awake at night

afraid I didn't use enough stone,
enough bone
afraid that if I let myself blink
it'll all come down on me
and break my heart in a way you never could

some considerations

You threw the clock at me when I came home
yesterday
Said you had cooked for me and I came home
late
I was thinking all day how to tell you
That although it was sweet of you to cook
The clock thing wasn't really justified
But then I figured you might throw a hot
spoon at me again
Saying fine you'll never cook again
I can go ahead and eat Panda Express
I can go ahead and get fat again
And then I'd think about it another day
How to tell you that I was never fat
I just gained a couple of pounds
Certainly not more than that
Then you'd throw the glass scale at me again
Saying fine I should leave you then
That you're so rude
So why should I stay with you
And I'd immediately let you know
That I love you so
That's why I work so hard—
And you'd stop me right then and there
Ask me to repeat myself
Ask me to explain to you
Why I think my job makes me better than you

And then before I can think
Of what to say
To make you understand that it's not okay
You'll be on me
Pushing me into the wall, *unintentionally*
Digging your fingers in deep
Leaving imprints so vivid
No concealer works on me
But it's okay
Because it's never the face
And you didn't mean it
But you apologize anyway
Buy me chocolates
And make me some cold lemonade

And I always think that's so considerate of you

cold mashed potatoes

We got married in August 1987
At least I think this is a marriage
You don't bother me much
I lost respect for you the first time you came home late drunk
Leaving me alone with the little ones
But I've made you regret it every day since then
With cold mashed potatoes

I'd made a mean pot roast
The day you asked for a sandwich instead
Ignoring all the hours I'd spent in the kitchen
You'd rather have cold meat on bread
But I've made you regret it every day since then
Stopped improving my cooking craft
Nowadays it's a costco chicken and some leftover rice

You started talking to the neighbor down the street
Getting yourself wrapped up in some scheme
Selling her piece of shit cars for her
You say it's just business
The babysitting gig I got going when you aren't home makes more

So does my little plant nursery
But you never invested in me
I could've been great
Greenest thumb in all of the gulf coast
My nursery would be the talk of the town still
Twenty years later
But you didn't want me to be a working
woman
So I clipped the coupons
Applied for food stamps
Soothing your ego along the way
Thinking your wages were enough to provide
for our four children
Wailing about
Washed their mouths out with soap
They never dared tell you a thing

But I've made you regret it every day since
then
The kids love me the most
Sure they've rebelled a few times
But nothing brings them running back faster
Than the quick crushing of their dreams by
your quick-witted tongue
Poor little ducklings never been stung
Still too young to realize how deep the hurt
goes

So
You'll spend your old days alone
And when you can't walk anymore they'll stick you in one of them homes
While I've got a round trip ticket to their vacations in Rome
I'll send you a postcard
Feel free to write me a letter
How's the view?
How are the potatoes?

arguments on the kitchen floor

arguments on the kitchen floor
we roll and we roll
till its 2am and we cant get back up anymore
I ask why you do this
you say you just can't help it
we're two little pill bugs
clashing over a principle
neither of us cares to uphold
"I'm yours, I'm yours"
that kind of currency doesn't work anymore
I want you to say you are wrong for this
you want me to say I'm just being a bitch
neither will break the curse
so we stay as two little pill bugs
clashing over a principle
neither of us cares to uphold

when chaos was my lover

she was no ordinary lover
she was chaos
have you ever kissed chaos?
she was sleepless nights and madness
she escaped from pandora's box
she visits me in my sleep still
to tell me how much better her life is without
me
and eviscerate me
so do not speak on her
do not ask me to compare
do not beg me to choose
between dreams of her and you

blank 30

my indifference pisses you off
but you forget the girl
that once believed in true love
did you care for her?
take into consideration her words?
don't blame me for the person that you made
melted me down
molded me like clay
and now we're asking ourselves different questions
you wonder if there's hope for us yet
I'm thinking that you gave me back two good legs

so why do I stay?

death of a button

I slip my fingers through your buttoned shirt
and pull
The threads snap and three buttons fall to the ground
You act like I've stabbed you in the chest
Like I've committed an act so violent
Broken the rules, sown the seeds of unrest

But I didn't start this war

I tell you to blame the seamstress instead
For not sewing on buttons strong enough to withstand the wrath of a tortured woman
Whose subtle begging never did her any good
You have trapped me in this falsehood
That you have done everything to change
That love does not lose to pain

The hand of the clock makes another round
In the midst of these affairs you always fail to make a sound
Moving lips and words so common, I can no longer distinguish them from the hum of the refrigerator or the whir of the fan

I finally understand

I stop fighting, and you think you've won
I pick up your buttons and sew them back on
I apologize for the things I've done wrong
And for the one button I cannot find,
The button that was lost

lonely nights together

I spent the night convincing myself that your meandering eyes
still meant I was your centerpiece, your queen
not reduced into interchangeable slabs of flesh
undressed again, there it is, the question on my lips
you bring me to my knees revealing that truly anyone will do
and I don't know if it's broken the spell or the curse
I just know it makes me feel so much worse

our history

the wrong side of history is where you don't
remember me
sobbing uncontrollably
prickly pear
you broke my heart
it almost feels like you punched my chest
fractured it, so delicate
feels like a violent fight went down
feels graphic, more pronounced
but it was a storm of words that came through
this town
echoes of past fights that knocked down the
light poles
flickering lights, incandescent, led the way
now our choices lead us astray

forgive me, I fell in love with you

the night I was set free
time stood still, curiously
I loved you
but you tore me in two
for sport
everything you believed
laid at my feet
my delusion ended by your own words

I am a shell
with wheels
I can roam the lands endlessly
but I don't bother
because all I can feel
is the cavity in my soul
I think it's a feeling that'll never go away
so I build a humble abode
the place where I will die
where I can forget myself
forget time
but most importantly
forget the boy that bankrupt me
took every last ounce of me
drained every emotion
then gave me a fuck you potion
when I asked for relief

sometimes the morning light hits my face
and for a brief moment I'm in a happier place
where silver linings line all of our skies
and we don't shackle ourselves with family
ties
but then I blink twice, clear the goop in my
eyes, and think back to the times I let you back
in
when you made yourself small,
when you showed me your wounds,
when you needed me
in those brief moments I loved you more than
anything
and I'm ashamed to say I would have never
walked away
because if it weren't for your own callous
nature
cutting me loose, letting me go, pushing too far
with your words
unable to comprehend
there could be a last time I found myself back
to you
there could be a path I took where I
contemplated too long,
and when I looked back,
my trail of footsteps would be nothing but
whispers in the sand

oklahoma-kansas line

at the oklahoma-kansas line
one suitcase lies atop the gravel of a parking lot
he went to get cookies and wine
and she left him a hundred dollar bill,
crammed it in there with every hope, wish,
and dream he promised to her
the only thing she kept
was the pain and the hurt,
permanent scars,
she can't tear off

his god might want for her to forgive him
to drive up north to be the mother of someone
else's child
call his affair a blessing and annihilate the last
bit of her soul
and from her ashes raise a family she'll never
belong to
whilst her own family had already gone and
fed her to the wolves
so there's no way forward and there's no way
back

except her god wasn't going to let her think
like that

engine running, feet thumping, a cold blast of air
she'll never forget how large, how immense her fear
overshadowed by the faint intoxicating idea
that living could be freedom
she jumped into the driver's seat before she could even finish the thought
and let her hair down for the first time in months

brave little fucking soul
venturing into the unknown
presses down hard on the gas pedal
windows down
going 90 on an open road
hair whipping around wildly
she could hardly see the road
could hardly see anything
but a future that belonged to her

my name

you curse my name
said all the love you had for me
fought my battles, died in vain

you say I'm dead to you
buried me in hollywood cemetery
on a nice hill, one last courtesy

you never mention my name again
never think back to the time
you begged me to stay
never see my back as I walk away from you
saying I've had enough of you
never hear the last words
that I wrote to you

because I kept them in a journal
kept my well wishes to myself
preserved every good thing I ever thought
about you, every good memory
in blue ink
on paper
every year the pages turn more yellow
every year I revisit it less
and when I'm gone it might last a little longer
but time gave me comfort, *once*
told me everything I know eventually turns to
dust

THE ONES THAT NEVER LEAVE THE HARBOR

keep you up at night

I have lost

I have lost my patience somewhere on the bus
that didn't stop for me
And I have lost all sense along with my
inhibitions
The day you refused to look my way
And I lost the need to speak the truth
When you drove out to the west coast
Leaving feelings unresolved
Your last image of me
Wasn't the most flattering
And I stalk the summer streets
Once covered in snow
I walk past your townhome, your front porch,
where all hope was held in the little fist that
knocked upon your door
I have lost
There isn't a moment in time where our paths
cross again
It's a somber lonely feeling
I have lost
But for you
I'd turn back time
To say the same words
Carve my place in your soul
Love like I've never loved before
And lose all over again

crushed ice

oh I picked a fight over you
with my hometown sweetheart
said you're just a friend
holding onto my sweet heart
while he lives his life a thousand miles away
kissing girls in museums
and threatening unspeakable things
if I ever refuse to see him

oh you'll tear me in two
just a wish wash of you
I'm your secret keeping colosseum
spending my days wishing I was yours
giving signs you choose to ignore
running back to a broken love
cause he was my best friend once

oh you think me pathetic
say this is life and I'm wasting it
you hold me close
I smell the alcohol on your breath
and I'm almost tasting it
dim light, midnight, smeared halloween
makeup
you whisper six words
then time stops for us
and the chance is there

I regret not taking it

it was never going to be me

in the midst of trying to light matches on fire
as I played matchmaker for you
I caught a spark of something I've felt a
handful of times before
sparks I know damn well I should've ignored
but you're always going to be something more,
unattainable and pure

I hid my feelings at the bottom of an ice cream
cake
and I've still got the pictures of us all singing to
you
smile so wide, it was all a ruse to get her in the
same room
you blew out the candles but your wish didn't
come true
so I spent the next few months foolishly trying
to make myself into that wish for you

but it was never going to be me
longing glances, taking chances
missed romances in the september rain
you held my hand and you held me close
and I'll always be amazed at how you loved me
so
enough to let me go

when you understood something about me I'd
yet to discern
when love like this felt like something I didn't
earn

but foolish girl that I was
I'd follow you into every room
the music always leading you to someone new
and I'd watch you all night
watch as you made yourself into a fool for
another
and though your eyes never failed to meet
mine from across the room
I knew I could stay waiting forever
to be the one you'd choose
but it was never going to be me

once more

Forever young, naive, and insecure
Starving for something more
Thinking we're forever doomed
To a future of heartache and solitude

We revealed our broken hearts to each other
And figured out
How to stitch them back together
While everything we'd never be
Was just meaningless ash at our feet

To be bold and in love
Let me do it over
Give me more time
To mess it all up
From the start
Take the kiss I never stole
And cement the undeniable

what you don't know

I bet you don't even know
that somewhere out there
in the big expanse of the world
this little speck in the universe
there is someone with such strong feelings for
you
they don't sleep at night
pass through blue bridges, mountain ridges
close their eyes
and see your face every time

she's got my heart

She's got my heart locked up in a shoebox
underneath her bed
Sitting amongst the pennies and books that
have never been read
I've knocked on her door more times than I
care to say
But she's never going to open it anyway
So
I grow a new heart
Pluck it straight from the sycamore tree that
long ago was embedded in me
I think it'll make for a good Christmas present
It sparkles underneath the moonlight, pure
and crystal-like

I knock on your door
Eager and secure
But I'm met with a panic in your eyes
Nothing you've bought is right
How will she ever love you
If you can't get this one thing right

Lovesick fools, we're nothing new
I tell you I've got just the thing
Just to see the brightest smile to ever exist

So now this new girl's got my new heart
Sitting next to her kitchen alarm
And it watches over you as you visit her house
instead of mine
Kiss her lips and drink her wine
Tell her stories of your wrongs, your rights
I get the luxury of hearing a first hand account
of how deeply you fall for her
Over and over again
And now I've got a dozen hearts
Scattered in a dozen homes
But not a single one sitting in my own

memory of you

It's new year's eve
And I've closed my eyes for the night
First you came in whispers
Sat behind me in the movie theater
I was too focused to notice
But then you stopped the film reel altogether
Said you could show me somewhere better
And you kept your promise
Took me to an indescribable place
I can't make out when I'm awake
But I know I must return every night
Cause it eases the nerves and the aches
And since then I'm just the woman who lives
in her dreams
Slips her fingers through reality's seams
To make the journey to an undisclosed location
To get tangled up in the sweet elation
Of irrationality
To laugh in your company

I can't remember the day you left
I can't remember why it is our time together
had to end

But I remember you

lost lovers

I think I fell in love with you the night you said
goodbye
You held me close, you held me tight
I was crying, it was a mess
But I felt it then, you held me like a lover
would, not like a friend

I spent the next year looking for you behind
bookshelves, beneath bottles of wine
I needed one last moment with you
One last chance to speak the truth

I found you sitting by a wishing well
One summer afternoon
You spent the evening telling stories,
and the night entangled in my hair
I held you close, I held you tight
Like you once did long ago, in the middle of
the night
I never felt more alive
And I could've kept this feeling, kept it my
whole life
But coward that I was, I let you slip through
my fingers
I had it all, now it's just the taste of regret that
lingers

something real

I wanted to call you
I wanted to tell you I was going to end it
A three year relationship isn't worth it
If every day feels like I'm dying
But you were just a wish that didn't come true
So what could I really say to you
I have to give him credit where credit is due
In my lowest moments,
he never left me stranded like you
Running away from the inkling of a real
feeling
Only able to articulate what I mean to you
when you're drinking
Nothing about me changes just because you
found the bottom of the bottle
Nothing about me changes when you're
suddenly sober
But you only want me when I don't feel real
When the future doesn't exist
And we're trapped in a moment without
consequence
When the things you say to me and the things
you do to me
Don't make me fall for you harder
Don't make me love you deeper

a star from above

A star fell from above
The night we fell in love
And the night sky was never the same

So why did we pretend to be?

Lily's Song

Lily watches me
As I slip the love of her life's hand in mine
We're off to the movies
Then to a late night drive
It's a new moon tonight
And I don't mind the darkness
Or the bullfrog's croak across the countryside
I keep my eyes on the stars
As he whispers promises to me

Lily's at home crying in the bathroom
Picking petals one by one
She laments not disclosing her feelings
Now her love is long gone
Lost in the arms of another
Someone much louder much bolder
She didn't think he'd go for a girl like me
She didn't think he'd go for another girl at all
Not after everything they've shared
Two kindred souls not yet formed into a love affair
But she was sure they would get there

I am the disruptor
And I see right through her
Cause once I was her
And if she didn't hate me so

Maybe I'd think about it, let him go
So she can swirl around in her feelings
Never quite revealing what he means to her
A gentle soul that never judged her
Held her in her darkest moments
And when she tried to push him away
He always stayed
To catch her teardrops before they fell
And if only she had asked him to kiss the pain away
She wouldn't feel the need to clutch her chest, discard rest, and let the river run the night
With her pent up hurt and spite

Smile
The worst is when she must smile at me
Tell me how happy she is that he is happy
Cause she's a good friend
She's his best friend
He's given her his time, peace of mind, and wondrous secrets
She could never betray him so
She must endure this falsity alone...

But it's Lily's Song
And I've got it all wrong
Crushing petals into poetry

It's the hope she gets high on
She whispers lies into his ears
Derailed my story I fear,
We are not alike
The garden snake has a bite

He comes to me
Says he's had a talk with you
The girl who knows him best
And he sees your point of view
All of it, how together we're a mess
So I bid my farewell
Then find you eavesdropping
At the foot of the stairwell
Smug smile, sparkling eyes
You ask who do I think I am
Deciphering people like anagrams
You tell me you've won
You sing your song

But I let you know that ten years down the road
It'll have been me who shared with him
Everything you only dared to imagine
And you'll only ever be Lily
of Lily's Song
Who got it all wrong
Because the most you'll ever have is a drunken kiss

He won't remember
And an invitation to a wedding
in November
I'll be somewhere warm, sun-kissed, wishing
him my best
While you sit sour-faced in a lilac bridesmaid
dress
Will you toast to his new wife's success?
Will you buy his kids gifts for Christmas?
All the while plotting your revenge
How long will Lily's song go on?
Before you abandon ship
And realize it's not worth it
Fellow fool can't you see?
You'll only ever have him in dreams

I kissed a boy

I kissed a boy
in your field of view
he was nice and sweet
but I didn't get his name and number
cause I was too busy chasing you
chasing you all the way down fifth avenue

and you say you saw nothing anyway
so why am I sitting drunk on your steps
feeling as sober as I'll ever be
asking you to look at me
and tell me
if I could ever be something you need

your mouth gives me the same answer as
always
but it's your eyes that never lie
and I take comfort in the simple fact
that at least it wasn't all in my mind
that my love and its foolish tendency to
survive
wasn't lost on the wrong one this time

the message

when this is all over

will you remember what you promised me?

when it's ten years down the road

will you think back to the time I wouldn't fall asleep?

I gave you every secret and thought that came to me
To fend off the fatigue that threatened to pull me in deep
Hoping time would decide to favor me and stop entirely
Morning would never come
and I wouldn't have to watch you go
Morning would never come
and we wouldn't have to grow old
To think back to this day ten years down the road
I don't think you'll remember what I said

But did you get the message?

blank 41

is it really true?
that you never knew?

if it were up to me

I traded diamond rings
for a couple of minutes in your dreams
and if it were up to me
we'd never leave
this short sliver in time
where our paths crossed

the fury of the snow

amongst the fury of the snow
lit brightly at midnight by the incandescent
bulbs,
nipping at my nose,
I swore I could've mistaken it for a gust of
orange fireflies
coming down to match the flutter of my heart
reminding me of the beauty of a short life
I forgot why we were waiting at that bus stop
but I still remember how your eyes smiled for
me
and I was always a dreamer,
but I can still pinpoint the moment you
brought me back into the real world
like somehow the present could be better than
anything I could've ever imagined
because we were talking and I was so happy
as happy, I thought, as I would ever be
just being in your company
and it was your single dimpled half smile
that made me question
why I ever settled for less
made me think I'd let you break my heart a
thousand times into a thousand pieces
and let that moment be the last time I took one
last cold breath
before I ever took back what I said to you next

THE ONES THAT ALMOST MAKE IT

hurt the most

rocky places

I found you one day in the forest sleeping atop
a smooth flat rock
That's when I realized no choice was ever my
own
Because I'm not lucky enough to stumble
down a rabbit hole,
Multiple, seemingly endless rabbit holes,
And find you

I never noticed the things I gave up to break
the fall
It was easier to think I was never missing
anything at all
Until I found myself within the quiet green
that surrounded you
And that's when I knew I was so much more
than a wandering creature holding on to past
lives
Counting time, tallying crimes

It took a handful of your words for my
cornflake breaded crust to crack
And I never sealed it back
I let the roots that sprouted at my feet
entangle me for an eternity
Because I never needed to to be anywhere else
again

the little pang

The little pang comes on days the sun sets
leaving that pinky orange trail behind

I get this feeling that I'll never see you again,
that forever is not meant for us, that I'll have
to witness these rare glimpses of beauty alone

I fear I will roam and roam and roam searching
for anything in life that compares to the
dreams we dreamed together

a quiet song

you call me when you need me
the house is on fire
you lit the flame
but you're an easy crier
you wanted it gone
now it's burning so slowly
and it hits you
as you're watching it closely

everything that hurt you
was all you had left of her
you can burn down the house
but you can't burn down her words
and in her absence they echo
so you sit and you beg for more
beg for more words
a letter, a note, an indication
of your worth

but you get no response
it's just you and me and a void no one will ever
be able to fill again

blank 57

I write this story in my head
Always rewriting
Everything but the end

what we inherit

two acres of land and a crumbling blue home
cracked overworked hands that had never
known warmth
cruel words that in our quietest moments echo

you're afraid you've nothing to give
to children you could call your own
but cold hard buckets of gold
you've spent a lifetime collecting
and lessons you never wanted to learn
that you'll spend a lifetime forgetting

you're afraid the things your father gave to you
is all fathers can pass on
you're afraid that as hard as you'll try
all it will take is one slip of the tongue

but I think I know you better than anyone else
to say
it won't be that way

in your darkest moments you are kind
even when you crack, you shine
take the opportunity to give a little piece of
you
to those who never deserved knowing you

the world will step on you, and you will thank
them
misinterpret their slight for acknowledgement
cause you've got a skewed sense of other's
good intentions
I worry that if I'd never met you
you'd keep mistaking the sharp end of a stone
for love

so no I don't think you'd ever harm a soul
with words that were never your own
you'd never tell a creature it is unwanted
and make sure that even when you're gone
they stay haunted

I love you

Say it again
it's 3am
but I need you to say it again
Say it until it's so ingrained in my brain
that even when I lose my mind
this feeling stays

Say it again
it doesn't matter if I close my eyes
it doesn't matter that when I wake
you'll be gone
it doesn't matter
that the world is not different
that in the grand scheme of things
we are insignificant

Say it again
all that matters
is that you say it again

blank 62

what if it's me bringing you down
what if when the clock strikes twelve
and I've reverted into the pumpkin that I am
the universe suddenly rewards you
for all you've had to endure
what if lack of me is the cure
cause you're holding on so tightly
gazing into me so intently
as you exclaim boldly
that it's not water leaking into our ship
that we're not sinking, but if we were sinking,
we're really not sinking that quickly
oblivious
you beg me to be oblivious
play along, sing that song
from that girl I used to love
tell you stories of her and him and every other
misguided whim
recite their soliloquies
re-enact how they buried me
spend the night living in memories
this feels like a memory

why is it all starting to feel like a memory?

Traitor!

you refuse to take my secrets to the grave, put
all my unresolved feelings on display
Traitor!
you've become my mother's favorite child
tell her about my schemes making it seem like
I'm amounting to something
Traitor!
you have a pleasant conversation with my
father about the time he used to work picking
tomatoes
Inexcusable! Reprehensible! Indefensible!
Traitor!
you push me to say something, say anything
you won't let me die with my fury and my
spite reflected in my eyes,
sewn deep in my heart
please,
promise me we'll never part

somewhere someplace

somewhere someplace is a home we deserve
where the self imposed curse has never been heard
and the things that keep us apart
burn with envy

the 3am haze

your childish delight always sizzles at the faint
whiff of strife
and your mind, grander than the great library
of Alexandria, so easily succumbs to
overbearing thoughts of what we are, what
we'll become

and then there is I, always overestimating my
resilience, promising to carry this weight for
the both of us
but I slip and I fall and I cry behind closed
doors hoping one day I wake up so small, this
burden cannot be mine anymore

our love is delicate and pure and in the coldest
of times reassures
that dark nights end and scars can mend and
every hurtful word we've kept, is something
we can forget

so how can I live without it?

a broken promise

if I am to spend the rest of my life
timing the snaps
to know when you would break my heart next
then so be it

I used to think I only loved you when your feet
were planted firm on the ground next to me
but I cannot forsake any part of you
my hands were made to be the cups
that catch the deluge that overruns you

if my life's sole purpose is to anchor you
to give you a life you think is worth living for
then say no more
it is yours

I rummage, I rummage

I wake in the middle of the night
to beg you to hold me close
the blue glow of the television light
is not enough to keep these dream eating
thoughts at bay
that say the ghost of me could've found a way
a pillar of perfection, the image of my parents
she never let anyone down, humbly wore the
crown
today I am half the woman she is
made small by knowledge
I rummage, I rummage
for love, for purpose

happiness

happiness was something you held in the palm
of your hand
slipped between the tips of your fingers
I was never going to win that battle
I was burden, I was misery, I was real
and I could try my best to change my nature
change to be what you needed
but I couldn't be that existential feeling
you chase when the world loses color but still
keeps spinning

I couldn't take the fear away

I look for us
deep in your eyes
but I see nothing there
something so certain
gone in the heat of the moment
it was always going to be like this
almost felt like I wrote it into existence
a hard feeling
but it's just acceptance

sucker-punched

sucker-punched, love this young wasn't meant
to come undone
now these unsung feelings break at the tip of
my tongue
and the twisted minute elicits unbalanced
ripostes
engrossed in thoughts, provoked by costs
who gets what, who gets lost
I become a relic of a different time
when you didn't need rhyme or reason
to just love me

the ledge

upon the ledge where you once bled
holding onto the one thing no one ever said,
you sit again
I tried to yell out, but my body failed me
hands to my chest, lack of breath
every word I wanted to say
tried to come out at the same time
and decided to choke me to death

and now I spend eternity with your demons
as they mock me
because they never once doubted their hold on
you
and now I'm just the little ghost that whispers
in your ear
senseless things that you can't hear

I notice that you never visit my gravestone
is it because you don't miss me?

now that I've left you alone
you found life is better without me?

in the quiet
do you find what it means to be happy?

a whim, a memory, a scar

not sure what twisted storybook we're living
in today
but I just wanted to say the way your eyes
shone in the moonlight
the night you told me I was forever yours
will haunt me for decades to come
so don't fear you'll be like the rest
a whim, a memory, a scar,
a thing I wished for upon a star
you are the home I will long for
every night we are apart
you are the eighth wonder of the world
imprinted upon my heart
warmth and smell
I could close my eyes
lose my eyes, lose every part of me
and be at ease with your warmth and smell
and though time threatens to take that too
the love and comfort I found in you
I know it will take every memory and all my
best days
set what I swore to others I would never forget
ablaze
before it takes away the love I have for you
you're the one thing I never want to lose
but I always lose
so just know I never lied to you

I will *always* love you.

parting words

and so we part ways amicably

that was a lie

the most vivid dream

the most vivid dream I had, I had with you
it was a dream so vivid it was almost a
memory
no,
it was a memory but with a different ending
my eyes were closed,
sand in my toes,
head in your lap,
your fingers tangled in my hair
I heard the waves crash into the rocks in the
distance
you held a seashell to my ear
then in the other whispered you were glad I
was here
and I cried
the rain this time came from inside
as I broke down in your arms
told you I didn't like who we'd become
and it all changed from that moment on

two broken souls made a home
learned love isn't just a promise on a piece of
paper, long forgotten
it is what it always was
the one thing missing from your childhood
home

the one I spent a lifetime looking for in brown
eyes, so similar to my own
the filling and the adhesive to a punctured soul
in my dream I do what I never did
let go of the past and exist
let go and let love win
I become what you need
because I loved you more than anything
because I tore myself apart for lesser things
because I always knew what your answer
would be
if I let myself be vulnerable, just once more
for the right person at the right time
maybe if you saw that strength in me
you'd want to get the help you need
and I wouldn't be lost in nightmares
afraid that in the end
loving you meant nothing

so in my dream
I ask you to forgive me
for leaving you in your darkest moment
for breaking when you believed me
unbreakable
I ask you to be patient with me, please
I ask you to never leave

and before I go on
you seal my lips with a kiss
say my request is unnecessary
nothing in this world
could ever make you leave me

I awoke blanketed in nothingness
Stone cold, almost dead
But my warm tears came
When reality set in
My heart broke
In a way it never had before
And I thought time would stop
But I was able to breathe again

THE ONES SAILING IN THE DARK

find themselves lost on their own

I break my every bone in hopes you hear the snaps

but your head is a thousand miles beneath the sand
or lightyears past the moon
I don't think you know the difference
after singing the same childish song proved futile
and sinking to the bottom of the ocean brought nothing
I thought if there was one thing I could give
to keep your eyes on me
then pain needn't be misery
but I slip by you swiftly
I'm ash in the wind
deposited in a past memory
a locked box of lullabies, woes, and wails
all cries for help you're unable to piece together
long ago I was young
and in a moment of shame I pushed you away
when all you wanted to do was rescue me
somehow that meant I had to lose you forever
how could my hurt hurt you so deeply
that you hear my call, leave me weeping

she's the girl you want to love

she's the girl you want to love
with a family that'll take you in with open
arms
she doesn't hide what she is
doesn't change for anyone

I jump at the sight of my shadow
at the thought of speaking to anyone
I think all the love I've had to give is all gone
I tried to buy more, refill my reservoir
but the ad in the brochure was just a scam
took my money then told me to be happy as I
am

so I went to go find a star to wish upon
only to find them all drowned out by the muck
of the city lights
I spotted a planet and made a wish anyway
but it's just like me, can't be what it isn't
even when all you want is to be different

all of this to say
thanks for the flowers, but you've got the
wrong girl
the one you want is down a couple of doors

old knots

we're both too old to pick fights
so I sabotage my life, my career
wondering if there really is nothing left here
and every time I think I'm over it
I've gone and built something I can be proud of
you put together the smallest string of words
and you crumble it
because my pursuits are fruitless
but you never taught me what is worthwhile
and every reincarnation of me
is a shot in the dark
because I don't know you well enough
to be sure the new version of me
is the daughter you always hoped for

I'm too old to cry
but you never look at me
never acknowledge the pain in my eyes
and you can claim to go blind
but my voice still quivers
you can hear the rivers

you're too old to hold onto this grudge
but you won't let me mend this bridge
master of words, every hurtful word I've used
I've learned from you
now you blame me for your wounds

I'm sorry
I'm sorry
you never taught me the concept of an apology
but I'm sorry

I need you now
I've needed you my whole life
but I need you most now
you can take back your twisted crown
you can keep your legacy
I've never wanted for anything
just please forgive me.
please talk to me
please say anything
because our only coping mechanism is one and the same
swallow the hurt and the blame
let the knot grow and ten years down the road
wonder why things are the way they are so
but my god can't you see that won't work anymore

we're just much too old

bubble tea

tethered to a forgotten land
I leave my footprints in the sand
awake in headaches
never asleep
as if forever waiting for a solution to come to
me
I drink happy tv
watch happy tea
bubble bubble
bubble over
four leaf clover
rabbit's foot
beg the good luck to come to me
don't leave me stranded
in sorrow island
where enemies lurk beyond the palm trees
bitter thoughts forming shapes that can hurt
me
some luck come to me
some luck, *please*

blank 59

you can hate me if you want
but I had to be selfish
pieces cannot pick up pieces
now who is there to stop me
from visiting the ledge you frequent

open secrets

sometimes wild hearts burn themselves out
sometimes diving in leaves more than bruises
and scars
the thought that taking risks doesn't pay off
still wrapped in the same muslin cloths
breaks more than one heart
hurt sinks deeper than my bones
a wound more persistent than any other I've
ever known

and I'm in the thick of it
guardian crickets
keep me in the same bleak state of mind
and that's how she finds me
my mother who tells me to tough it out
no need to be weak and cry
about how the world has long since left me
behind
why can't I learn to be like her
all happy and smiles in the face of loss and
hurt
and that's when I snap at her
I yell like I've never yelled before
and on another occasion
I might have felt shame more
but I don't hold back
I tell her I know she cries

alone she goes out and hides
like a hurt animal who thinks it's about to die
and I tell her how I wish she wouldn't pretend
that she's content with her life
that a husband need not be a friend
and a thirty year relationship can't end

my mother cries
I try, I apologize
I tell her she never let me feel comfortable in
my own skin
so how could I share with her my deepest
secrets
why would she ever assume she could be
someone I could seek comfort in
when she's so keen on telling me what I can
and can't do
when all my choices contradict her worldview
she asks when I'm getting married all the time
how do I even begin to have that conversation
about love lost and depression
about someone so peculiar
my whole existence was in question
how do I take advice from someone
I'm not even sure knows what that kind of love
is
she'd give it all for her children

but what about the man she's decided to spend
the rest of her life with
how can she help me
when I have been consumed by another soul
when all I am left with are words
frame them, shape them, disintegrate them
they seep out through the pores of my skin
words too painful to keep within

I find silence
my outburst is not welcome in this household
I speak her language but she does not
understand me
the voice of reason does not reason with me
had I been a different sibling
maybe she'd have tried
but she just holds me
and I understand that we cannot have it all in
this world
mothers who comprehend and lovers who stay
but I do live to see another day

blank 2

I am a pressure cooker
About to blow up
But the relief never comes

playwright

I am vapid I am vain
I am the villain in your play
You mock me so others may mock me too
Gives you a sense of worth in your solitude

I'd accuse you of stealing scenes from my life
But honestly I don't think you got it right

Cause you can’t come up with anything more demeaning
Than the things I write and say about myself
Maybe if you were a better storyteller you could peel back the layers
Aim for the heart and get a fuck you card sometime in December

the worst thing

the worst thing you can say to a girl
is that you love her
so why do I do it over and over
kiss her and promise the world
so I don't have to spend this time alone

the worst thing you can say to a girl
is that you love her
because when you tell her you'll change for her
she believes you
she's decided I'm the pathetic little project
she's going to restore
and I can't find it in myself to tell her that
truly there's no hope

the worst thing you can say to a girl
is that you love her
because even if you want it to be true
some things just can't come to you
she's hanging onto the ghost of me
reads my longing poetry
and has convinced herself we're meant to be
and I just can't find the words to tell her
everything I am today is just a falsity
and she deserves better, so much better
I just can't find the words to tell her

she doesn't love you

You're her consolation prize
A beautiful wedding
Paid by your parents
A house in the hills
Vacation in the villa

You're her consolation prize
But you know that right?

I may be a bitter old witch
But I still have eyes
I see how you see her
The image of perfection
Composed and refined
She gives you her polite smile
Her "let's get this over with" smile
Reserved for events
With your family and friends
Reserved for time alone
With you
But you remember how she was with him
A devilish grin and a spark in her eyes
A spark you wanted for yourself
Attention you craved
You swooped in when he left her for that girl upstate
And it's her bitterness that ties her to you

The rage within that holds her together
Keeps her so outwardly mundane

I know I know
Who the fuck asked me
I'm just the local cynic
Popping bubbles cause I can't go back to my own
But trust me when I say
That woman's only in it for the brownstone
Cause a picture perfect life
A well-preserved lie
Goes a long way these days
To ease the pain, bleach the brain
Why ponder love lost
And the why every time you turn a corner
Why not just forget hands on hips
Tongue on lips
Candlelit promises
And act like you got everything you ever wanted instead
Become this whole other person
That knows what happiness is
You might be an empty shell
But as long as no one else can tell
There might be a point in time
Where you won't know the difference yourself

you're in love with me

I wonder how many years it's been
I wonder how many years it took
For you to realize
Everything you loved about him
Was just me
Late night texts,
Asking advice on work, on men
He'd ask me what to say
Never had an original thought in that brain
Your favorite restaurant was my
recommendation
And if I'd have stuck around
I'd have picked the damn ring too
You would have liked it better
Because I know all about you
Because your deepest secrets are in my
lockbox too
You'd think he'd at least have the emotional
bandwidth to deal with you
Cause he never did shit for me
But no
Did you hear my poem in his words?
Just listen a little more closely
Play the tape again
Do you see?
You're in love with me
But don't worry

Maybe the next girl will fall in love with the
taste of cherry from your lips
And say your signature scent is hers now too
She'll get your gifts for Christmas
She'll be oblivious
The most interesting thing about him was us

the apathetics club

I never knew I could be as cruel as those who
came before me
dangling my sanity by the thread of their
unrelenting apathy
of course they broke my heart
if living means nothing
and I was never special enough to spark
something in them
to make the world start spinning again
they'd gut me like a fish just to see if they'd
feel any different
now I gut others too
and I've got to say
it's not even thrilling

things get better

relax they say, things get better
but I'm holding my breath
and I don't feel lighter
the chip on my shoulder gets deeper
incessant thoughts grow bolder
I'm nowhere near the end
so why does it feel like it's over

flowers in my hair

A little fairy landed on my lap
One cool spring morning
I'd stayed up the night before
Solemnly drinking on the back porch
I'm almost certain I dreamed her

She reprimanded me as she began to place the tiniest of flowers in my hair
Says I've been terrible, I've been bad
I go around spreading doubt and misery across the land
In places where she's sprinkled hope
I've meddled in her territory
Screwed up her love stories
I've undone her hard work

Now I'm not in the business of arguing with fairy tale creatures
And I had a bunch of other questions on my mind
But her comment irked me
I've only *ever* been kind

I ask the fairy if she's ever loved
She's taken aback
Says no, never experienced a thing like that
But her little saddened eyes betray her

I laugh
It's a cruel thing to laugh
But I laugh

Look at you flitting around
Playing matchmaker, conjuring up gowns
You comfort others with words you wish to hear
You comfort others to ease your fears
I know, I've been there
You paint them a picture
of how you wish the world would be
Cause if it works out for them,
you start thinking,
hey, maybe it'll work out for me
Little fairy thing chasing an ideal
Fly away now
You won't find the next Cinderella here

I expected the fairy to give me a disapproving glare
Instead there is a softness in her eyes, a look of understanding
She tells me it is a beautiful thing to be human
And I almost pluck off her wings
When understanding turns to pity

I try to look away
But there's too much pride
And now I'm entrapped
Reflected in her eyes
I see what they all see
I cannot help it, I crack

I'm growing old
With nothing real to hold
Everything I've ever loved is dead or dying
I still hold on to the last tuft of fur my white rabbit ever shed
I still feel the burn from the sun that once gave me warmth
I'm not even thirty yet and my damn bones hurt
Not from the change in the weather
but from the weight of everything I never said
to everyone that deserved better

But before the fairy can reply, I wake up
It's mid-afternoon, the pit in my stomach's still there
And there's no flowers in my hair

farewell firefly

you weren't supposed to be like the rest of us
forever running in circles
because we like the feeling of doing something
but changing nothing

pick up your bags, turn back around
it's not too late to take a ship, take a plane
follow that little bit of you that drives others
insane
and never return, this isn't home

I know it feels all wrong
but you can get it right again
won't you get it right again?
do it for us nonbelievers
you can make us dream again

let me write your happy ending

blue skies
and a happy new wife
let me write your happy ending
as a way for me to apologize
I haven't been myself lately
I wonder if I was ever myself at all

you get everything you worked for
all those years struggling to get by
you finally get their respect
you no longer cry in parking lots
at 3am with the girl who told you one day
it wont matter how much it hurt
it'll be like those aesop fables
it'll be like folklore

I know you'll ask why it's not me by your side
just know you tried and you tried and you
tried
I was always what you wanted
and I have to be honest, I never figured out
why
but I thank you and I thank you and I thank
you
til the end of time
I made you my family
and I'll never take that back

but you build a new family
and you're never alone again
hiding under bed covers
reliving what was said
cause the best part is
words never hurt you again

barefoot on cobblestones

It's cold, from the lack of touch
and lack of physical movement
The blanket is two steps away
but she's picked a comfortable position
One of her better decisions
A never ending string of words that won't let
her sleep seeps in
She hasn't spoken in weeks
But she keeps herself company
And she's kind of funny
The stream keeps on running
It used to be all more vivid in her head
Little things of note she never could have said
Little things that made her happy and
Little hurtful words that in her heart she kept
She tosses, she tumbles, til it's midnight and
something inside her has clicked

First she stumbles, then she runs
Out of the cocoon that's imprisoned her for
months
Chases the empty streets for the rush of a
feeling, any feeling
She settles for skin on stone
ache in the bone, lack of breath
and a smile for no one to witness
only for her to hold

THE ONES IN STILL WATERS

find clarity in solitude

I took some time

I took some time off in the winter
So I could go pity myself
Took a hit of nostalgia
So I could wonder where the years went
And feel the passing of time in my soul

A bucketload of pennies, a wishing well, and
me
I'd have better luck at the coinstar
Skip hapless wishes for grocery gift cards
Guess I'm a chance taker
Emptied the copper like liquid gold
And felt no different

Sometimes it feels like I've done it all
But truthfully all I did was fall
Back into the same person
Who did everything to change
But remained the same

a whisper in the wind

I sit and wonder sometimes
if I'll ever see you again
but I know the truth
it'll be reliving a death
when
my heart is already six feet underground
and the rest of me burned at the stake
my bones blended
the person you held
is a whisper in the wind
the pollen that irritates your nose
gives life, blooms a rose

I am an afterthought
but I do exist
in those quiet moments
where you reminisce
of days you thought were long forgotten
and feelings you don't feel too often
you close your eyes
and unwittingly whisper in the wind
the words we never said to each other

museum of broken hearts

I gave it all for the moment I could be able to
look around
and be comforted by the things you couldn't
take away
your collection of broken hearts might contain
mine
little broken thing frozen in time
you collected the pieces for display
that's your image of me
little broken thing left in the driveway

but I've long since outgrown
that shell that only held love within your
parameters
because I found the thing you promised me we
had
and I found it by chance
so rare it could never be held
in your two cent museum of oddities
trophies discarded by the once broken hearted

glimmer

friend,

don't go back to him
your worst memories
have been polished by time
a twinkle so innocent
pain becomes iridescent

friend,

you remember the rush
everything else not as much
hungover, leftover, impromptu sleepovers
yelling out his name in the middle of the night
catching the 2am bus ready for a fight

friend,

put the idea to rest
you may not yet know who you are
but you are no one's second best
come, get dressed
stand still in the middle of the room
spin once, spin twice

see

you don't need cheap tricks to glimmer

in between what came and went

you spooked me
made me believe I couldn't be who I wanted to
be
I used to sit and wonder all the time
how could I make someone so small my sky
you were my muse, I was your stepping stone
afraid to be left behind, afraid to be left alone

somewhere, in the midst of your affair
I saw all the things I wanted
the things that weren't there

and I let you go

good things came, good things went
but never again did I feel the need to spend the
night with benign lies
afraid to take a good look in the mirror, afraid
to look past the disguise
never again did I taste your flavor of regret
smeared on the inside of my cheek,
bitter and sweet

snout

I woke up one day with a snout
hands became large paws
and a heavy brown fur enwrapped me
I was still a two-legged creature
I remained this way for three solid years
taking time to catch and prepare meals
basking in sunsets and honey droplets
sleeping months at a time
I did not encounter another soul
except that of the chirping bird
and the smaller four-legged creatures
I guess really I just didn't encounter another
soul like me
starving, hungry, unwilling to be seen
focused on existing
delighted at the feeling of the creek over my
feet
terrified of the small talk that comes from
bumping snouts
and wandering about

in the end,
solitude was a wondrous friend

she

I might have heard a tale or two
spent younger days wishing they were true
and I might have expected to live the rest of
my life
not knowing the bittersweet taste of your
untimely demise

justice comes in many shapes and forms
oftentimes justice is not what we wish for
hurt minds bide time in more creative ways
no justice system dares embrace

but if you lived the rest of your life without
consequence
it would not have mattered to me
I put every thought I had of you to rest
I was content
simply never hearing your name again

but she came to your town one night
to return everything you had given out
a little basket of hurt and spite
broken promises and tears wept
stolen years filled with misery
left on your doorstep

some say you lit your own kingdom on fire
but the way the bridges burned
and your castle crumbled
was straight out of a fantasy
I couldn't have imagined myself

muse to the poet, feared by the wicked
she knows of everyone's affairs
endless time to refine her craft
it was the work of a weaver
and I don't know if she ever heard my prayers,
long since lost to the past

but I'm a believer

birds on telephone lines

I took a picture of this little bird
perched above me on a telephone line
It tilted its head, almost as if it had noticed me
I smiled
But it must have been the click of the camera
that miffed it so because it squawked at me,
said it knows me, sees me everyday sitting in
my back porch, all lonely

Where's your lover? Where's your family?

It asked all casually
I sighed, contemplated going inside
But then the little thing flew down and settled
onto my window, took a peek into my empty
home, then looked at me and said it really just
must know

Where's the pretty little butterfly that's been
following you around for months? Grew tired of
hanging out with the losers and the drunks?

Bird said it bet two worms and five cigarette
butts on me getting dumped before the end of
the month
I didn't answer the bird's question, only said

Why are you so judgmental?
I'm just enjoying my life

It's not like you've got it all figured out
You're just some bird sitting all alone on a telephone
line, gambling and people watching as a pastime

The bird chuckled, flapped its wings, then said

Yes but I can fly,
open my wings, anytime, say goodbye
So I'm not alone, I've got the whole world to explore

Annoyed, I quickly replied

Well I've got the whole world too
It doesn't belong just to you
I'll take a plane, no not a plane,
got a fear of planes
But I'll take a ship, any ship
and sail sail sail away!

bird tilted its head,
narrowed its beady eyes,
then said

Knowing you,
it'll be a ship that goes nowhere.

Then it flew away, cackling,
never to return
And I'm still mad about that comment to this
day.

after

I've carried a storybook in a locket
since the time I was able to form a feeling
from the stories woven by the little words
perched on paper, little words and their
unspoken meaning

You were afraid to never be enough for a
dreamer but you could never fit within the
pages of a storybook
You're the one chapter I cannot close because
you weren't written with pen and paper,
you were etched into my bones

I know how your story ends
Because I ripped up my dreams so you could
reach the fabled shores I've longed for
And I hope you never feel the need to pity me
A dreamer has endless dreams
But truly,
There isn't anything else I could ever want for

and so I was wrong

I believed if only I was brave
the thing I wished for most in my heart
would come true

whispers whispers

every weekend at six thirty am
an old man appears on a park bench next to
white oak bayou overlooking the misty city
skyline in the distance
his companion is rather new to the scene
a loyal dog, black with tufts of white
most days he walks alone, same jogging trail,
same wooden bridge
next to the same mossy pond
with turtles and creatures abound
an onlooker might see
an old man with a routine
no children, no wife
no anger, no spite
only the peace and solitude that comes with
old age

But whispers whispers tell a tale much less
simpler
Talk of the household
His children know his every move
How he walks the park,
feigning peace and solitude
The dog is new
Years in the making
A girl begging her entire childhood
For him to let her have a four-footed friend

Denied til she took matters into her own hands
Decided she didn't give a fuck
Now her dog stalks him loyally
And he grumbles about insignificant things
About how his daughter no longer listens to
him
No longer respects him
Makes himself oblivious, immune
To the tears she sheds
Sitting cross legged on his bed
Detailing her side of the story
Her tale of what's right and wrong
Her tale of how she's all grown up
It's not disrespect for him
But respect for herself
He doesn't understand the difference

She gives up for a time
Then decides to poke the bear again
67 with ways too immovable to break
It's a hurricane, It's an earthquake
She thinks this time will be it
Where she doesn't break down
Doesn't shed tears
Only hopes her love is enough
To get him to talk to her
Get him to notice her

Just because I make my own decisions
Doesn't mean I don't need you in my life anymore
Just because my path isn't yours
Smooth routine, dependable, and secure
Doesn't make it any less worthy to take

But it's futile
There's no justice, no change

Til one Sunday came
First time in his life
33 years of marriage, he confided in his wife
He doesn't know where he went wrong
If every child of his
Has got some sort of issue with him
And they talked about it
That day and every Sunday that came
He took her out for dinner
Held her hand
Walked with her through all his favorite paths
The little park, the fancy park with the waterfall, and the one the dog loved with the turtles and doves
Simple gestures were radical changes
And his daughter and him never did get on the same page
But she peered at her parents from afar

This new development in their relationship
Something she never expected to see
And a little piece of her heart healed
When she felt there might be hope for her
after all.

About The Author

Evelyn Avila is a Mexican-American poet and storyteller. She was born in a small Texas town in the middle of nowhere and has led a mostly uninteresting and bland life.

She lives alone in the big city with a medium-sized black dog she named after a constellation. Her coffee intake is average. Her goal in life is for people to read her writings. So if you have read this book, she thanks you.

Follow Evelyn on social media @eeviepoetry

www.ingramcontent.com/pod-product-compliance
Lightning Source LLC
LaVergne TN
LVHW090522110826
845146LV00003B/944

* 9 7 9 8 9 9 0 5 6 4 9 0 9 *